Collins
INTERNATIONAL

English Foundation

Activity Book B

Published by Collins
An imprint of HarperCollins*Publishers*
The News Building, 1 London Bridge Street,
London, SE1 9GF, UK

HarperCollins Publishers
Macken House, 39/40 Mayor Street Upper,
Dublin 1, D01 C9W8, Ireland

Browse the complete Collins catalogue at
www.collins.co.uk

10 9 8 7 6 5 4

ISBN 978-0-00-846857-6

British Library Cataloguing-in-Publication Data
A catalogue record for this publication is available from the British Library.

Author: Fiona Macgregor
Publisher: Elaine Higgleton
Product manager: Letitia Luff
Commissioning editor: Rachel Houghton
Edited by: Hannah Hirst-Dunton
Editorial management: Oriel Square
Cover designer: Kevin Robbins
Cover illustrations: Jouve India Pvt. Ltd.
Internal illustrations: Jouve India Pvt. Ltd.,
p12 Martin Sanders, p 18 Karen Oppatt,
p19–21 Sahitya Rani
Typesetter: Jouve India Pvt. Ltd.
Production controller: Lyndsey Rogers

Printed in India by Multivista Global Pvt. Ltd.

Acknowledgements

With thanks to all the kindergarten staff and their schools around the world who
have helped with the development of this course, by sharing insights and
commenting on and testing sample materials:

Calcutta International School: Sharmila Majumdar, Mrs Pratima Nayar, Preeti
Roychoudhury, Tinku Yadav, Lakshmi Khanna, Mousumi Guha, Radhika Dhanuka,
Archana Tiwari, Urmita Das; Gateway College (Sri Lanka): Kousala Benedict; Hawar
International School: Kareen Barakat, Shahla Mohammed, Jennah Hussain; Manthan
International School: Shalini Reddy; Monterey Pre-Primary: Adina Oram; Prometheus
School: Aneesha Sahni, Deepa Nanda; Pragyanam School: Monika Sachdev; Rosary
Sisters High School: Samar Sabat, Sireen Freij, Hiba Mousa; Solitaire Global School:
Devi Nimmagadda; United Charter Schools (UCS): Tabassum Murtaza and staff;
Vietnam Australia International School: Holly Simpson

The publishers wish to thank the following for permission to reproduce photographs.

(t = top, c = centre, b = bottom, r = right, l = left)

p 11tl Corbis/Ecoscene/Ian Beames, p 11bl Corbis/Kennan Ward, p 11br Alamy/David
Boag, p 14tl Africa Studio/Shutterstock, p 14tr Olga_i/Shutterstock, p 14cl Kwadrat/
Shutterstock, p 14cr jps/Shutterstock, p 14cl Vishnevskiy Vasily/Shutterstock, p 14cr
Africa Studio/Shutterstock, p 14bl jps/Shutterstock, p 14br Vishnevskiy Vasily/
Shutterstock, p 15t Vishnevskiy Vasily/Shutterstock, p 15b jps/Shutterstock

Extracts from Collins Big Cat readers reprinted by permission of HarperCollins
Publishers Ltd

All © HarperCollins*Publishers*

MIX
Paper | Supporting
responsible forestry
FSC™ C007454

This book contains FSC™ certified paper and other controlled
sources to ensure responsible forest management.

For more information visit: www.harpercollins.co.uk/green

Circle

Circle each of the fruits you like to eat.
Say the names.

Date:

Find and circle

 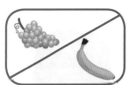

     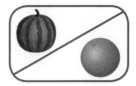

Follow the pattern in each line.
Circle what comes next.

Date:

Trace and say

apple

banana

grapes

melon

strawberry

Trace the first letter.

Date:

Trace and draw

I like

Trace the letters. Draw your favourite food.

Date:

Match

Match each home to who or what lives there.

Date:

Trace and say

boy

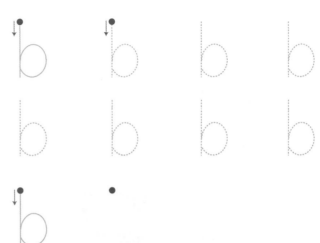

dog

Trace the letters. Say the sounds.
Try writing some more.

Date:

Circle

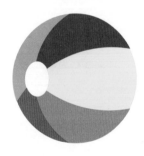

Circle the things that start with the 'b' sound.

Date:

Colour

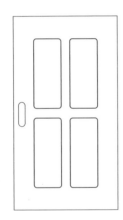

Colour the things that start with the 'd' sound.

Date:

Draw

Draw your favourite animal. Write its name.

Date:

Count

 **1 2 3**

1 **2** **3** **4**

How many animals are there?
Write the number for each group of animals.   Date:

Find

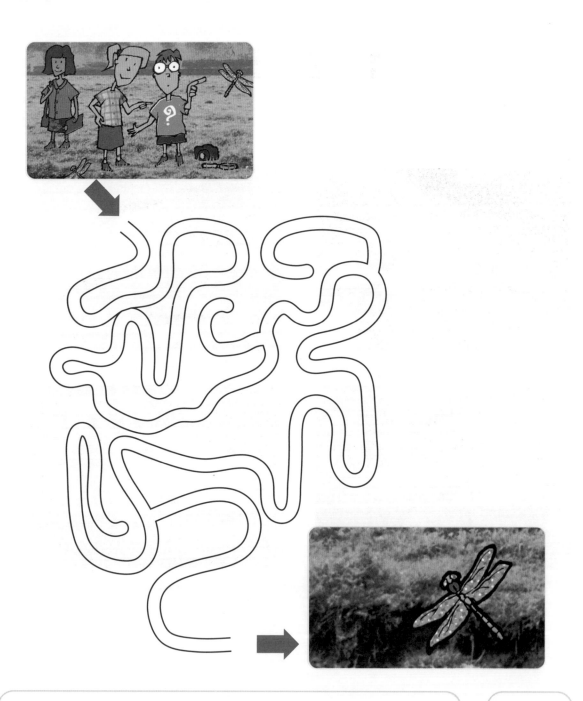

Help the children to find the dragonfly.

Date:

Follow

Follow the dots to trace the patterns from left to right.
Try drawing some more patterns.   Date:

Find

Help the grown-ups find their babies. Follow
the dotted lines. Use a different colour for each.   Date:

Put in order

1 **2** **3**

How do these animals change as they grow?
Put them in order. Number them 1, 2 and 3.   Date:

Write and say

_____

_____

_____

_____

_____

_____

Put a 'b' next to all the big animals,
and an 's' next to all the small animals.   Date:

Trace and say

baby

b b b b

b b b b

b

mother

m m m m

m m m m

m

Trace the letters. Say the sounds.

Date:

Tick

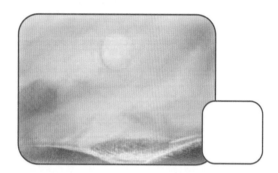

Tick what you can see at night.

Date:

Tick

Tick the things you do during the day.

Date:

Match

sam

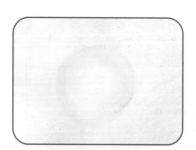

sun

mum

moon

Match each word to a picture. Trace the words.

Date:

Find

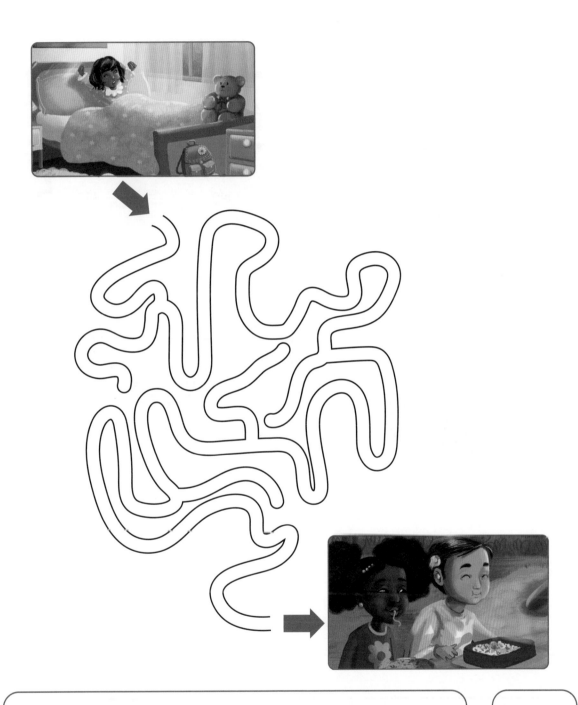

Draw a line and help Sam find her friends at school.

Date:

Alphabet time

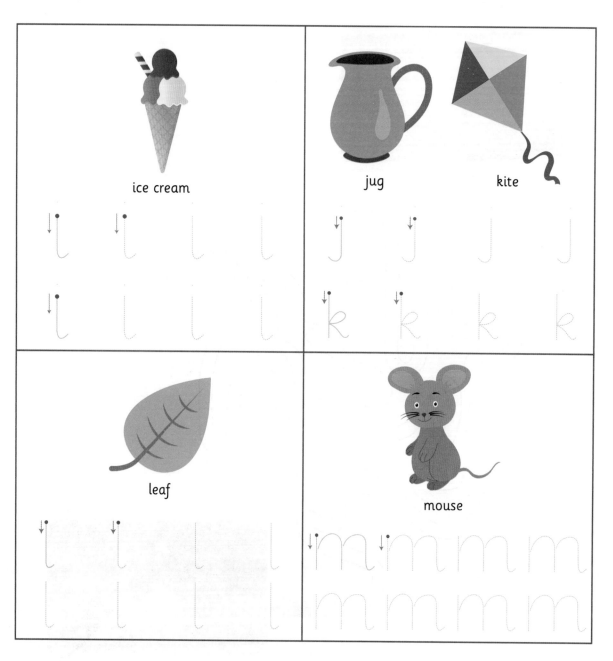

ice cream

jug

kite

leaf

mouse

Alongside structured phonics lessons, you may want to display and talk about one letter of the alphabet in an 'alphabet time' session each week.

Alphabet time

nest

n n n n n
n n n n n

orange

o o o o o
o o o o o

pencil

p p p p p
p p p p p

queen

q q q q q
q q q q q

Alongside structured phonics lessons, you may want to display and talk about one letter of the alphabet in an 'alphabet time' session each week.

Assessment record

_____ has achieved these English Foundation Phase Objectives:

Reading

R1 Become aware of sound structures in language	1	2	3
R2 Develop pre-reading skills	1	2	3
R3 Recognise some letters of the English alphabet	1	2	3
R4 Understand and explore the link between letters and the sounds they represent	1	2	3
Reading motor skills	1	2	3

Writing

W1 Develop pre-writing skills	1	2	3
Writing motor skills	1	2	3

Speaking

S1 Be able to express oneself in everyday situations	1	2	3
S2 Understand sentences	1	2	3
Speaking developmental skills	1	2	3

Listening

L1 Know how to listen and respond appropriately in everyday contexts	1	2	3
Listening developmental skills	1	2	3

1: Partially achieved
2: Achieved
3: Exceeded

Signed by teacher:
Signed by parent: Date: